NGINX Unit Cookbook
Recipes for Using a Versatile Open Source Server

Derek DeJonghe

Beijing · Boston · Farnham · Sebastopol · Tokyo

NGINX Unit Cookbook

by Derek DeJonghe

Printed in the United States of America.

Published by O'Reilly Media, Inc., 1005 Gravenstein Highway North, Sebastopol, CA 95472.

O'Reilly books may be purchased for educational, business, or sales promotional use. Online editions are also available for most titles (*http://oreilly.com*). For more information, contact our corporate/institutional sales department: 800-998-9938 or *corporate@oreilly.com*.

Acquisitions Editor: Mary Preap	**Indexer:** Potomac Indexing, LLC
Development Editor: Virginia Wilson	**Interior Designer:** David Futato
Production Editor: Christopher Faucher	**Cover Designer:** Karen Montgomery
Copyeditor: Piper Editorial, LLC	**Illustrator:** Rebecca Demarest
Proofreader: Piper Editorial, LLC	

September 2020:   First Edition

Revision History for the First Edition
2020-09-02:   First Release

See *http://oreilly.com/catalog/errata.csp?isbn=9781492078562* for release details.

This work is part of a collaboration between O'Reilly and NGINX. See our *statement of editorial independence* (*https://oreil.ly/editorial-independence*).

978-1-492-07856-2

[LSI]

Table of Contents

Preface

The *NGINX Unit Cookbook* aims to provide a reference for using NGINX Unit through practical real-world examples. Throughout this book, you will learn about NGINX Unit, its features, and where it fits in your system architecture. This guide will provide you with the knowledge to effectively use NGINX Unit and simplify your system architecture by using a single middleware server for a wide range of web application use cases.

This book will be most useful for system engineers, architects, and those in a DevOps role, whose position is focused on web application delivery, deployment, and security. A background in web application hosting and the HTTP protocol will help readers understand the concepts contained in this book.

Chapter 1 will explain the what and why of NGINX Unit, in a traditional report form, before transitioning to the how, in a cookbook format, for the rest of the book. The main focus areas will be installation of NGINX Unit, its configuration API, serving applications and routing requests, security and application isolation, and integration with common web languages and ecosystems.

I personally believe in NGINX Unit and have begun using it in my own web system architectures because of its versatility and simple minimalistic configuration. NGINX Unit enables me to deploy web application environments for a wide variety of use cases and language ecosystems effectively with a common middleware server. My hope is that the information in this book will empower you to do the same.

Conventions Used in This Book

The following typographical conventions are used in this book:

Italic
> Indicates new terms, URLs, email addresses, filenames, and file extensions.

`Constant width`
> Used for program listings, as well as within paragraphs to refer to program elements such as variable or function names, databases, data types, environment variables, statements, and keywords.

 This element indicates a warning or caution.

Using Code Examples

Supplemental material (code examples, exercises, etc.) is available for download at *https://github.com/dejonghe/nginx_unit_examples/tree/master/2020*.

If you have a technical question or a problem using the code examples, please send email to *bookquestions@oreilly.com*.

This book is here to help you get your job done. In general, if example code is offered with this book, you may use it in your programs and documentation. You do not need to contact us for permission unless you're reproducing a significant portion of the code. For example, writing a program that uses several chunks of code from this book does not require permission. Selling or distributing examples from O'Reilly books does require permission. Answering a question by citing this book and quoting example code does not require permission. Incorporating a significant amount of example code from this book into your product's documentation does require permission.

We appreciate, but generally do not require, attribution. An attribution usually includes the title, author, publisher, and ISBN. For example: "*NGINX Unit Cookbook* by Derek DeJonghe (O'Reilly). Copyright 2020 O'Reilly Media, Inc., 978-1-492-08723-6."

If you feel your use of code examples falls outside fair use or the permission given above, feel free to contact us at *permissions@oreilly.com*.

O'Reilly Online Learning

 For more than 40 years, *O'Reilly Media* has provided technology and business training, knowledge, and insight to help companies succeed.

Our unique network of experts and innovators share their knowledge and expertise through books, articles, and our online learning platform. O'Reilly's online learning platform gives you on-demand access to live training courses, in-depth learning paths, interactive coding environments, and a vast collection of text and video from O'Reilly and 200+ other publishers. For more information, visit *http://oreilly.com*.

How to Contact Us

Please address comments and questions concerning this book to the publisher:

O'Reilly Media, Inc.
1005 Gravenstein Highway North
Sebastopol, CA 95472
800-998-9938 (in the United States or Canada)
707-829-0515 (international or local)
707-829-0104 (fax)

We have a web page for this book, where we list errata, examples, and any additional information. You can access this page at *https://oreil.ly/NGINX-unit-cookbook*.

Email *bookquestions@oreilly.com* to comment or ask technical questions about this book.

For news and information about our books and courses, visit *http://oreilly.com*.

Find us on Facebook: *http://facebook.com/oreilly*

Follow us on Twitter: *http://twitter.com/oreillymedia*

Watch us on YouTube: *http://youtube.com/oreillymedia*

Acknowledgments

Special thanks to Ryan Tasson and Artem Konev for their detailed reviews and feedback.

Unit Introduction and Features

This chapter will introduce you to NGINX Unit in a traditional book format before switching to the O'Reilly Cookbook format in Chapter 2. Throughout this chapter, you will learn about what makes Unit different from other middleware application servers. Before learning the how, you'll learn the why, with a brief history of the problem Unit aims to solve. From that understanding, the architecture of NGINX Unit will be introduced, followed by the language support, and finally the API that drives the configuration.

1.1 Application Landscape and Unit Project History

The landscape of web applications has changed. In the past, applications were written from the ground up to serve specific needs, and upgrades were seldom issued compared to the present day. Today, applications are released frequently, in a piecemeal fashion, and portions are completely rewritten over time. As teams and web application offerings grow, the likelihood of the logic being diverse in both language and code base grows as well.

As web applications diversify through microservices, languages, and language versions, so does the operational complexity of managing middleware, where *middleware* is defined as the application server that receives requests and ushers them to the application code. Installing, configuring, tuning, and maintaining multiple types of middleware servers for different types of application languages and versions requires a lot of work, expertise, and time and affects the bottom line.

This solution, NGINX Unit, aims to reduce operational complexity by providing a single middleware server that is able to run multiple applications of different languages and versions and update on the fly without dropping a connection.

1.2 Dynamic Web Application Server

NGINX Unit is a dynamic web application server, which means that it can be dynamically reconfigured during runtime without dropping requests. The architecture of Unit is such that request handling is broken into layers. These layers comprise a controller process, a router process, and some application processes.

Each application served by Unit is run by an isolated process or set of processes. The router process receives incoming connections and asynchronously queues them for the destined application. The controller process manages the configuration of the application and router processes. The administrator, or operational automation, interacts with the controller process through an application programming interface (API). The controller process is able to reconfigure the router process and the application processes on the fly.

1.3 Polyglotism

Polyglotism is the ability to speak multiple languages. Prior to NGINX Unit, a few polyglot middleware services have served the web well—for example, the Common Gateway Interface (CGI) supports languages such as PHP, Perl, and Python; the Web Server Gateway Interface (WSGI) supports Perl, Python, and Ruby. Unit provides a single middleware server to run both compiled and scripting languages—including the aforementioned languages as well as Node.js, Go, and JSP—through a unified configuration.

With NGINX Unit, teams are able to code in the application language that makes the most sense for the service they're providing to the end user. This technology reduces the difficulty of running complex systems to enable business value from all aspects.

1.4 API-Driven Configuration and Server Management

The NGINX Unit controller process is advertised through an API. The API can be configured to be served through a Unix or TCP socket. These two options allow the API to be tightly controlled but also enable remote configuration. This API follows RESTful paths, methods, and JSON bodies, per industry standard.

The controller process is able to start and stop application processes and to reconfigure only necessary portions of the router process's memory. This ability to start applications and configure traffic routing accordingly is the core of the dynamic reconfiguration. These paradigms enable native integration with operational workflows found in DevOpsian organizations.

1.5 Conclusion

NGINX Unit has a unique place in system architectures, as it's able to consolidate the number of different middleware server types needed to run a polyglot system. When system engineering teams are able to standardize, they become much more efficient. Teams that are going through migrations or technology transformations and need to write configuration management for a number of different web application middleware servers should consider using NGINX Unit.

Unit is an excellent choice for applications stuck in traditional data centers. Its API and dynamic nature provide an overlay on static infrastructure that enables software and DevOps teams to drive change from the application layer. Cloud deployments also benefit from Unit, as the industry-standard API fits directly into the ecosystem, and its lightweight resource footprint and functionality diversity allow teams to get the most out of their provisioned infrastructure.

Unit is built for serving web requests. An example of when Unit would not be a good fit would be running asynchronous worker applications that feed off of a queue or message bus.

The rest of this book is written in O'Reilly's Cookbook format. The Cookbook format follows the cadence of problem statement, solution, and discussion.

CHAPTER 2

Installation

The first step for using NGINX Unit is installing it. NGINX Unit can be installed on a wide variety of systems. This chapter will detail how to install Unit on the major Linux distributions such as Debian, Ubuntu, Red Hat, CentOS, and Amazon Linux through NGINX package repositories. Other installation methods, such as compiling from source and using third-party repositories, are also included to enable success with NGINX Unit on virtually any Linux-based platform.

2.1 Red Hat–Based Systems (.rpm)

Problem

You need to install NGINX Unit on Red Hat, CentOS, or Amazon Linux.

Solution

Create a file named */etc/yum.repos.d/unit.repo* that contains the following contents:

```
[unit]
name=unit repo
baseurl=https://packages.nginx.org/unit/OS/$releasever/$basearch/
gpgcheck=0
enabled=1
```

Alter the file, replacing OS at the end of the URL with rhel, centos, amzn, or amzn2, depending on your distribution.

Install the Unit base package:

```
sudo yum install unit
```

Install additional modules that you may want to use with Unit:

RHEL-like systems version 6.x:

```
sudo yum install unit-devel unit-jsc8 unit-php unit-python
```

For RHEL-like systems version 7.x and 8.x, you must specify versions of some language modules:

```
sudo yum install unit-devel unit-jsc8 unit-jsc11 \
      unit-perl unit-php unit-python27 unit-python36
```

Discussion

The file you just created for this solution instructs the yum package management system to utilize the Official NGINX Unit package repository. The command that follows installs Unit from the Official repository, as well as the Unit modules needed for each application language you may want to run.

The official packages rely on default language versions that are available for the respective systems within the same package manager ecosystem. Information on customizing language modules can be found in the section Additional Resources.

Additional Resources

System Requirements (*http://bit.ly/2ISB4ss*)
CentOS Package Documentation (*http://unit.nginx.org/installation/#centos*)
RHEL Package Documentation (*http://unit.nginx.org/installation/#rhel*)
Working with Language Modules (*https://unit.nginx.org/howto/modules*)

2.2 Debian-Based Systems (.deb)

Problem

You need to install NGINX Unit on a Debian or Ubuntu machine.

Solution

Ensure that the Advanced Package Tool (APT) system is able to use HTTPS repositories:

```
sudo apt install apt-transport-https
```

Create a file named */etc/apt/sources.list.d/unit.list* that contains the following contents:

```
deb https://packages.nginx.org/unit/OS/ CODENAME unit
deb-src https://packages.nginx.org/unit/OS/ CODENAME unit
```

Alter the file, replacing OS at the end of the URL with ubuntu or debian, depending on your distribution. Replace CODENAME with the code name of your system. If you don't know the code name, the following command will output the value you need:

```
lsb_release -c
Codename:       xenial   # Example
```

Run the following commands to install the NGINX signing key and install Unit:

```
wget http://nginx.org/keys/nginx_signing.key
sudo apt-key add nginx_signing.key
sudo apt update
sudo apt install unit
```

A version of the language needs to be specified for certain Unit modules. At the time of this writing, not all versions of all languages are supported across all versions of the OS. You can search for module packages available from the repository for your operating system by using the following command:

```
apt-cache search unit- | grep NGINX
```

Install additional modules that you may want to use with Unit. The following packages are available on all Debian-based systems:

```
sudo apt install unit-php unit-python2.7 unit-perl \
     unit-ruby unit-dev unit-jsc-common unit-jsc8
```

Discussion

The file you just created instructs the apt package management system to utilize the Official NGINX Unit package repository. The commands that follow download the NGINX GPG package signing key and import it into apt. Providing the APT system with the signing key enables it to validate packages from the repository. The apt update command instructs the APT system to refresh its package listings from its known repositories. After the package list is refreshed, you can install Unit and any necessary packages from the Official NGINX repository. The search command demonstrated previously can assist in finding which language versions are available for your system.

Additional Resources

System Requirements (*http://bit.ly/2ISB4ss*)
Debian Package Documentation (*http://unit.nginx.org/installation/#debian*)
Ubuntu Package Documentation (*http://unit.nginx.org/installation/#ubuntu*)

2.3 Go and NPM

Problem

You need to install the Go or Node.js Unit packages for Unit to hook into your application.

Solution

Unit's Node.js package is called `unit-http`. It uses Unit's libunit library; your Node.js applications require the package to run in Unit:

```
sudo npm install -g --unsafe-perm unit-http
```

Unit's Go language module is hosted directly by NGINX. This module enables your Go application to communicate with the Unit router process directly:

```
go get unit.nginx.org/go
```

Discussion

NGINX maintains packages libraries for external applications types. These libraries must be installed for the respective application to be able to run in Unit. These examples show how to install the library or module for Node.js and Go with the default package manager for either ecosystem.

2.4 Third-Party Repositories

Problem

You want to run NGINX Unit on a system for which NGINX Inc. does not have pre-built packages, and you do not want to build from source.

Solution

Install from a third-party repository. These named repositories are maintained by the community; NGINX has no control over or responsibility for these resources.

Third-Party Repositories

These third-party repositories are maintained by the community. They may not contain the latest versions and can be subject to change.

Alpine Linux:

```
sudo apk update
sudo apk upgrade
sudo apk add unit
sudo apk add unit-openrc unit-perl unit-php7 unit-python3 unit-ruby
```

Arch Linux:

```
sudo pacman -S git
git clone https://aur.archlinux.org/nginx-unit.git
cd nginx-unit
makepkg -si
```

FreeBSD:

```
sudo pkg install -y unit
```

Gentoo:

```
sudo emerge --sync
sudo emerge www-servers/nginx-unit
```

Remi's RPM repository hosts the latest version of PHP for RHEL and its derivatives, such as CentOS and Fedora:

```
sudo yum install --enablerepo=remi unit \
    php54-unit-php php55-unit-php php56-unit-php \
    php70-unit-php php71-unit-php php72-unit-php php73-unit-php
```

Discussion

This section has detailed the usage of a number of third-party repositories maintained by the community. It is possible to utilize this information to quickly install prebuilt Unit and Unit module packages on systems that NGINX Inc. does not yet maintain a repository for. Also, the Remi repository contains specific older PHP versions that may be useful to some readers.

Additional Resources

System Requirements (*http://bit.ly/2ISB4ss*)
Community Repositories Install Documentation (*http://bit.ly/2GH0TKE*)

2.5 Installing from Source

Problem

You need to install Unit from source code.

Solution

You will have to install the packages needed to compile from source. The following includes all the development packages for all supported languages; skip the packages that you are not going to use.

For Debian and Ubuntu:

```
sudo apt install build-essential
sudo apt install golang
sudo curl -sL \
     https://deb.nodesource.com/setup_<Node.js version>.x \
     | bash -; apt install nodejs; npm install -g node-gyp
sudo apt install php-dev libphp-embed
sudo apt install libperl-dev
sudo apt install python-dev
sudo apt install ruby-dev
sudo apt install openjdk-8-jdk
sudo apt install libssl-dev
```

For Amazon Linux, CentOS, RHEL, and Fedora:

```
sudo yum install gcc make unzip
sudo yum install golang
sudo curl -sL \
     https://rpm.nodesource.com/setup_<Node.js version>.x \
     | bash -; yum install nodejs; npm install -g node-gyp
sudo yum install php-devel php-embedded
sudo yum install perl-devel perl-libs
sudo yum install python-devel
sudo yum install ruby-devel
sudo yum install java-1.8.0-openjdk-devel
sudo yum install openssl-devel
```

In some cases you may need to install the Go programming language repositories, Perl itself, and the following packages: `gcc-c++`, `perl-ExtUtils-Embed`.

Clone or download the source code from *https://github.com/nginx/unit*. If you choose to download, you'll need to unzip the package that is downloaded. Once the source is cloned or unpacked, move into the base of the project. The next example follows the download path:

```
curl -O https://codeload.github.com/nginx/unit/zip/master
unzip master
cd unit-master/
```

Alternatively, you can download the source directly from NGINX:

```
curl -O https://unit.nginx.org/download/unit-1.18.0.tar.gz
tar xzf unit-1.18.0.tar.gz
cd unit-1.18.0
```

You can update the version number, in the event you're looking for a newer version of Unit.

Next, use the `configure` script to prepare the source code for installing on your system. Run `./configure --help`, or `./configure <language> --help`, to fully understand the flags available. In the following example, the `--prefix` option is used to specify the installation directory. Each supported language has an associated module that also needs to be built. Run the `configure` script with each application type you need to build a module for:

```
./configure --prefix=/opt/unit/
./configure go --go=/usr/local/go/bin/go
./configure perl
./configure php
./configure python
./configure ruby
./configure nodejs
./configure java
```

Next, use the `make` command to run the *Makefile* created by the `configure` script and install the software. You will need to run the `make` command for each language. Each language has its own configuration options. Depending on the location and ownership of the `--prefix` flag specified by the `configure` command, you may need to run the last command with elevated privileges:

```
make
sudo make go-install
sudo make node-install
sudo make install
```

NGINX Unit is now installed. Validate the installation by getting the help options from the binary:

```
sudo /opt/unit/sbin/unitd -h
```

Discussion

The preceding steps will build and install NGINX Unit from source. A number of configuration flags can be used to modify the build and installation. Unit is ready to use.

Additional Resources

System Requirements (*http://bit.ly/2ISB4ss*)
Source Installation Documentation (*http://bit.ly/2GtKNCC*)

CHAPTER 3

Configuration

There are three main types of configuration objects used by NGINX Unit. All are defined with JSON. The application object defines characteristics of the application being run by Unit, such as the language, the process controls, and the location on the filesystem. The listener object defines the Unit configuration that directs incoming requests on a defined IP address and port to a specified application. The route objects provide routing capabilities. The routing capabilities include routing to Unit applications, serving static files, proxying to external services, and load balancing over a pool of servers. This chapter will build a foundational understanding of these objects.

3.1 Application Object

Problem

You need to understand the application object for a fundamental understanding of NGINX Unit.

Solution

Define an application object that describes an application on the system. Each application type has different attributes and options that can be applied. The following is a basic example of a PHP application object:

```
{
    "applications": {
        "my-app": {
            "type": "php",
            "processes": 2,
            "root": "/var/www/app/",
            "index": "index.php",
            "user": "app_user",
```

```
                    "group": "app_group"
            }
        }
    }
```

Discussion

Every application deployed on NGINX Unit is defined by an application object. The application object, defined in JSON, specifies the application's attributes. Each application type has its own required and optional attributes. A number of different application attributes control Unit process management and limitation. The `type` attribute is the only process management attribute that is common and required across all applications; it defines the application language, such as PHP, Python, Golang, Ruby, or Perl. Other attributes include application process count limits; time limits; user, group, and environment variables; and working directory.

In the example, some of the attributes that can be applied to a PHP process are used, such as `root` and `index`. The application-specific attributes are focused on the entry point of the application, such as the directory of the project or the main executable file.

The `processes` option shown in the example is set to a static number of 2 application processes. Optional attributes `max`, `spare`, and `idle_timeout` are also valid for process control. The `max` and `spare` attributes represent an integer of the maximum number of processes and number of spare processes to keep on hand, respectively. The `idle_timeout` attribute represents the number in seconds a process can stay idle before being killed if there is an excess of the number of spare processes.

You will learn how to apply application objects to the Unit configuration in the section Recipe 4.2.

Additional Resource

Applications Object (*http://bit.ly/2IImvbG*)

3.2 Listener Object

Problem

You need to understand the NGINX Unit listener object in order for your application to listen for requests.

Solution

Define a listener object to instruct Unit to listen for incoming requests on a provided IP and port:

```
{
    "listeners": {
        "*:8080": {
            "pass": "applications/my-app"
        }
    }
}
```

Discussion

To instruct NGINX Unit to listen for incoming requests, a listener object must be defined. The listener object defines the application to which Unit will direct incoming requests. The listener object is the value, specified to a key that defines the IP and port. In the example, the * is used for the IP address, thus instructing Unit to listen on all IP addresses assigned to the server. The listener object has two attributes: pass and optionally tls. The pass attribute takes a string value that specifies the application, application target, route, or upstream to which requests will be directed. The example sends requests directly to an application named my-app.

You will learn how to apply listener objects to the Unit configuration in the section Recipe 4.2.

Additional Resource

Listeners Object (*http://bit.ly/2DzbB3w*)

3.3 Route Object

Problem

You want to understand the NGINX Unit route objects to enable internal routing between listeners and applications.

Solution

The routes attribute of the Unit configuration can be configured as an array of route steps or an object of named route arrays.

When an array of route steps is used as the value of the `routes` attribute, the value provided to the `pass` attribute is simply `routes`, as in the following example:

```
{
    "listeners": {
        "*:8080": {
            "pass": "routes"
        }
    },
    "routes": [
        {
            "match": {
                "host": "blog.example.com"
            },
            "action": {
                "pass": "applications/blog"
            }
        },
        {
            "action": {
                "pass": "applications/my-app"
            }
        }
    ]
}
```

Figure 3-1 depicts this simple routing example. Route steps are evaluated in the order of their appearance.

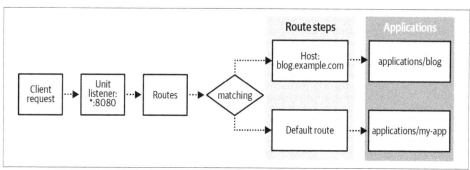

Figure 3-1. Simple NGINX Unit routing

When an object of named route arrays is used as the value of the `routes` attribute, the value provided to the `pass` attribute must be `routes/` followed by the named route, as in the following example:

```
{
    "listeners": {
        "*:8080": {
            "pass": "routes/main"
        }
```

```
    },
    "routes": {
        "main": [
            {
                "match": {
                    "host": [ "example.com", "www.example.com" ]
                },
                "action": {
                    "pass": "applications/website"
                }
            },
            {
                "match": {
                    "uri": "/admin/*",
                    "scheme": "https"
                },
                "action": {
                    "pass": "applications/admin"
                }
            }
        ]
    }
}
```

Figure 3-2 depicts the routing of a scenario that merges these two route configuration examples, naming the first example route blog.

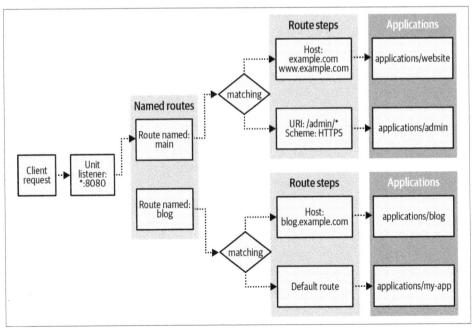

Figure 3-2. Named NGINX Unit routing

Discussion

This recipe demonstrates a couple of basic routes. A route step has two attributes: match and action. Both attributes have their own respective object types that have a number of configurable attributes.

The match object has the following options: arguments, cookies, destination, headers, host, method, scheme, source, and uri. With these options, you can identify a web request and direct it to the correct action. The only valid values for scheme are http or https.

There are two types of match options: simple and compounding. The following are simple match options: destination, host, method, source, and uri. These options match against a string pattern or an array of patterns. When specifying multiple options together in a single match object, they work as a logical AND. When an array of strings is used for one of these options, the match at the option level is evaluated as a logical OR.

A pattern can use wildcards, negations, or ranges. Wildcards (*) prefixing, suffixing, and splitting the string are valid with the host, method, and uri match options, as well as the IP portion of source and destination. Negations (!) are also supported, but they must come at the beginning of an option value. Ranges, in the format {start_port}-{end_port}, are supported for the IP and Port portions of the source and destination options. The option values patterns must be an exact match to the request for the action to take effect.

Compounding match options use an object of key-value pair attributes to define a match. The following options use the compounding match: arguments, cookies, and headers. To match a request for a compounding match option, the request must match all of the attributes of the option. The key attribute names the particular argument, cookie, or header your request is trying to match. The value of the attribute behaves exactly like a simple type match option, accepting a string pattern or an array of string patterns.

The action object takes the following options: pass, share, fallback, proxy, return, and location. The pass action type routes the request to a given route, upstream, or application, where the share serves static content from a given file path. The fallback action is used in conjunction with a share to reroute the request in the event a file requested is not found or cannot be accessed. Routes can be chained for more complex logic. The proxy type will proxy the request to another HTTP server. The return attribute alone will return a status code. To redirect a request, the return and location attributes can be used together to return an HTTP status code and a redirect location.

The route steps in a given array are evaluated in order, and the first match takes action. If only the action attribute, but no match condition, is specified in a route, requests are unconditionally directed to the pass, share, or return value. If no route is matched, an HTTP 404 is served.

Additional Resources

Route Object (*http://bit.ly/2Dx0dpc*)

3.4 Proxying

Problem

You need to proxy a request handled by Unit to another HTTP service.

Solution

Use the routes attribute of the Unit configuration to specify a route object that uses a proxy action type:

```
{
    "listeners": {
        "*:8080": {
            "pass": "routes"
        }
    },
    "routes": [
        {
            "match": {
                "uri": "/wiki/*"
            },
            "action": {
                "proxy": "http://172.17.0.1:80"
            }
        },
        {
            "action": {
                "pass": "applications/my-app"
            }
        }
    ]
}
```

This example routes any request with a prefixed URI of /wiki/ to an external HTTP service hosted at http://172.17.0.1:80, and all other requests to an application hosted by Unit.

Discussion

The proxy action type will relay the request to an external HTTP service. The capabilities of this action are that of a basic reverse proxy. You can use Unix, IPv4, and IPv6 socket addresses as targets. This Unit feature will fit many use cases. For more advanced features, you may look to the NGINX reverse proxy and load balancer server.

Additional Resources

Route Object (*http://bit.ly/2Dx0dpc*)

3.5 Static Files

Problem

You need to serve static files with Unit.

Solution

Use the `routes` attribute of the Unit configuration to specify a route object that uses a `share` action type:

```
{
    "listeners": {
        "*:8080": {
            "pass": "routes"
        }
    },
    "routes": [
        {
            "action": {
                "share": "/var/www/static/",
                "fallback": {
                    "share": "/var/app/static"
                }
            }
        }
    ]
}
```

This example serves all requests out of a local file directory, */var/www/static/*. If the file is not found, Unit will fall back to an alternate location, */var/app/static*. When serving static content, a `user` attribute is not specified as it is with applications. The files are accessed with the access rights of the user Unit runs as, usually root.

Discussion

The share action type will serve static content from a local directory. It can be used in conjunction with the fallback action, which will tell Unit how to direct the request if the requested file is not found or if Unit has insufficient privileges to access it. The fallback action can route requests to a pass, proxy, or share action. When fallback directs requests to another share action, the fallback actions can be nested.

Additional Resources

Route Object (*http://bit.ly/2Dx0dpc*)

3.6 Upstreams/Load Balancing

Problem

You need to load balance over multiple servers external to Unit.

Solution

Use the upstreams attribute of the Unit configuration to define a pool of servers to load balance over:

```
{
    "listeners": {
        "*:8080": {
            "pass": "upstreams/pool-0"
        }
    },
    "upstreams": {
        "pool-0": {
            "servers": {
                "10.0.0.2:8080": { },
                "10.0.1.2:8080": {
                  "weight": 2.0
                }
            }
        }
    }
}
```

This example will load balance between servers 10.0.0.2 and 10.0.1.2, both of which listen on port 8080. These two servers are defined as an upstream named pool-0. The server at 10.0.1.2 will receive twice as many requests as 10.0.0.2 because of the weight attribute.

Discussion

The `upstreams` attribute of the Unit configuration defines a number of named upstream objects. Each upstream object defines a `servers` object. The `servers` object uses keys to define the destination and uses the value to specify an optional `weight`. The upstream uses a weighted round-robin load balancing algorithm. The maximum `weight` value is 1000000, the minimum is 0 (such servers receive no requests), and the default is 1.

The load balancing capabilities of Unit are pretty basic but fit many use cases. For more advanced load balancing features, you should use the NGINX reverse proxy and load balancing server, which is described in Chapter 7.

Additional Resources

Upstreams Object (*https://unit.nginx.org/configuration/#upstreams*)

3.7 Targets

Problem

Your application has multiple entry points, and you need to separate routing, root directories, and the index or script being run.

Solution

Use the application attribute `target` to provide a separate context within the same application:

```
{
    "listeners": {
        "*:8080": {
            "pass": "routes"
        }
    },
    "routes": [
        {
            "match": {
                "host": "admin.example.com"
            },
            "action": {
                "pass": "applications/my-app/admin"
            }
        },
        {
            "action": {
                "pass": "applications/my-app/website"
            }
```

```
            }
        ],
        "applications": {
            "my-app": {
                "type": "php",
                "targets": {
                    "admin": {
                        "index": "admin.php",
                        "root": "/var/www/admin"
                    },
                    "website": {
                        "script": "index.php",
                        "root": "/var/www/"
                    }
                }
            }
        }
    }
}
```

Discussion

This section took the route and application configurations to a deeper level. The application configuration has an attribute, targets, that defines another layer of application context. A PHP application must have a root and script or index attribute defined at either the application level or a target level. In the example, the admin target has a different root directory than the website target. The admin target also allows all PHP files within the directory structure to be called, with admin.php being the index. The website target contains the admin root directory; however, it only allows for the *index.php* script to be called. Up to 254 targets can be configured for an application. Routing to a target is done by simply appending to the application namespace with the name of the target.

CHAPTER 4

Usage and Operations

Understanding how to start and stop the NGINX Unit server, and the applications it runs, is essential. In this chapter, you will learn how to start and stop the Unit service on init.d and systemd service managers, as well as how to start the Unit server in the foreground. This chapter also details how to submit the configuration objects to the Unit control API in order to start serving the application.

4.1 Startup and Shutdown

Problem

You need to start or stop the NGINX Unit server.

Solution

When Unit is installed through a repository, a startup file for a service manager such as init.d or systemd is also installed and configured. These service managers will start Unit as a daemon.

Start Unit on an init.d system:

```
sudo /etc/init.d/unit start
```

Stop Unit on an init.d system:

```
sudo /etc/init.d/unit stop
```

Start Unit on a systemd system:

```
sudo systemctl start unit
```

Stop Unit on a systemd system:

```
sudo systemctl stop unit
```

Start Unit in the foreground. The following assumes that the Unit binary is installed into a directory defined in your PATH:

```
sudo unitd --no-daemon
```

Discussion

The service manager used to start the Unit daemon depends on the type of system it's running on. Each service manager has its own syntax for starting and stopping services. The service managers will start Unit as a daemon. An example of starting Unit in the foreground is also shown. This can be useful for testing or when running Unit in a Docker container.

4.2 Applying Configuration

Problem

You need to alter the NGINX Unit configuration through the control interface.

Solution

For this section, it's important to understand that the Unit configuration is represented as a single JSON object. Portions of the object can be interacted with in a RESTful manner. The following are examples of working with specific application and listener objects, and then with the Unit config as a whole.

Locate the Unit control socket; example output is provided. The default value found in this example, /var/run/control.unit.sock, will be used throughout the book. As the control socket is owned by root by default, all curl commands will be run with sudo:

```
unitd -h

unit options:

   --version            print unit version and configure options

   --no-daemon          run unit in non-daemon mode

   --control ADDRESS    set address of control API socket
                        default: "unix:/var/run/control.unit.sock"
   ...
   ...
```

Create an application by submitting an application object to the control socket:

```
sudo curl -X PUT -d @/path/to/application-object.json \
    --unix-socket /var/run/control.unit.socket \
    http://localhost/config/applications/my-app
```

In accordance to REST standard, a PUT request overwrites prior configurations that might have been previously defined for a given entity.

Configure a listener to send requests to the application:

```
sudo curl -X PUT \
    -d '{"*:8080":{"pass":"applications/my-app"}}' \
    --unix-socket /var/run/control.unit.socket \
    http://localhost/config/listeners
```

Figure 4-1 depicts the routing at this point.

Figure 4-1. Simple NGINX Unit configuration

Configure a route object named `main` to match `/wiki/*` and serve static files from `/var/www/static/`:

```
sudo curl -X PUT \
    -d '{
      "main":[
        {
          "match":{"uri":"/wiki/*"},
          "action":{"share":"/var/www/static/"}
        }
      ]
    }' \
    --unix-socket /var/run/control.unit.socket \
    http://localhost/config/routes
```

Append specifically to the route array named `main`, with a POST method to the `routes/main` entity, that will direct all other traffic to the application:

```
sudo curl -X POST \
    -d '{"action":{"pass":"applications/my-app"}}' \
    --unix-socket /var/run/control.unit.socket \
    http://localhost/config/routes/main
```

Set the listener object to direct traffic at the route, rather than the application:

```
sudo curl -X PUT \
       -d '"routes/main"' \
       --unix-socket /var/run/control.unit.socket \
       'http://localhost/config/listeners/*:8080/pass'
```

Figure 4-2 depicts the routing at this point.

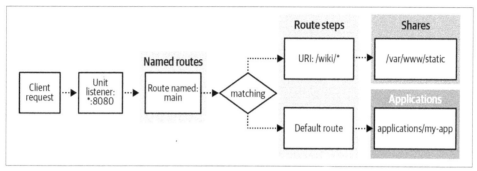

Figure 4-2. Simple NGINX Unit configuration

Use the GET method to retrieve and save the entire configuration to a file named *config.json*:

```
sudo curl \
       --unix-socket /var/run/control.unit.socket \
       http://localhost/config/ \
       -o config.json
```

Your `config.json` file should look similar to the following:

```
{
    "listeners": {
        "*:8080": {
            "pass": "routes/main"
        }
    },
    "routes": {
        "main": [
            {
                "match": {
                    "uri": "/wiki/*"
                },
                "action": {
                    "share": "/var/www/static/"
                }
            },
            {
                "action": {
                    "pass": "applications/my-app"
                }
            }
```

```
            }
        ]
    },
    "applications": {
        "my-app": {
            "type": "php",
            "processes": 5,
            "root": "/var/www/app/",
            "index": "index.php"
        }
    }
}
```

Alternatively, you can create all of these objects at once by applying the entire configuration file with a PUT method:

```
sudo curl -X PUT -d @config.json  \
     --unix-socket /var/run/control.unit.sock \
     http://localhost/config/
```

> This command removes all other listeners, apps, and routes that might have been defined previously.

Test your application:

```
curl localhost:8080
curl localhost:8080/wiki/somefile
```

Discussion

All interactions with Unit are done through the control interface. The API is RESTful; applications and configurations are created, altered, or deleted through the API. In the examples for this solution, we build on the examples from Chapter 3 by submitting them to the Unit control interface. Throughout the example, you created an application, a listener, and a route. You then updated the route and the listener. By using a GET method, you retrieved the entire configuration of the running NGINX Unit server and saved it to a configuration file. Finally, you used the returned configuration file to set all configurations at once with a single HTTP request to the control interface.

It is important to note what each HTTP method will do to a given entity targeted by the API RESTful endpoint. A GET will return the configuration or value for a targeted entity. A PUT will set the configuration or value for a given entity, overwriting what was previously configured. A POST will append to a configuration array. A DELETE will delete the entity and return a status message.

4.3 Limits

Problem

You need to limit the number of requests an application will process before being respawned as well as the amount of time it has to respond before timing out.

Solution

Use the `limits` option of an application object:

```
{
    "listeners": {
        "*:8080": {
            "pass": "applications/app-name"
        }
    },
    "applications": {
        "app-name": {
            "type": "php",
            "processes": 5,
            "root": "/var/www/app/",
            "index": "index.php",
            "limits": {
                "timeout": 10,
                "requests": 10000
            }
        }
    }
}
```

Discussion

The `limits` option takes an object that is comprised of one or two options. The `time out` option configures how long in seconds NGINX Unit will wait for a request before timing out and returning an error to the user. The `requests` option defines how many requests an application process can serve before being restarted. Restarting a process after a certain number of requests is helpful for applications that have memory leaks.

CHAPTER 5

Security

Security is everyone's job. NGINX Unit enables many layers of security configuration. Unit naturally separates applications by spawning separate processes for each one, enabling isolation at the process and memory layer. Each application process can be owned by separate users, enabling security at the file permission layer as well. Each application can also have its own Linux namespace specifications. Next, NGINX Unit has full SSL/TLS support, which enables Unit to serve applications through encrypted HTTPS communication. Finally, the system user accounts that are used to run Unit (the account that the unitd daemon runs as, the control socket owner, and the app-specific user and group accounts) enable fine-tuning access rights. All of these security attributes are demonstrated in this chapter.

5.1 Unix User Permissions

Problem

You need to further isolate your applications by using user permissions.

Solution

Use a different system user for each application so that Unit spawns the processes as separate users with their own permissions:

```
{
    "applications": {
        "auth-service": {
            "type": "ruby",
            "working_directory": "/var/app/auth/",
            "script": "/var/app/auth/config.ru",
            "user": "auth-app"
        },
```

```
        "key-service": {
            "type": "external",
            "working_directory": "/var/app/key/",
            "executable": "bin/key-app",
            "user": "key-app"
        }
    }
}
```

Discussion

Unit runs each application as a separate process or group of processes, enabling it to run these processes as separate system users. When configuring an application in Unit, there are attributes for user and group. Using separate system users for each application will provide your applications with further isolation. The example demonstrates two different applications running as separate users in two separate working directories. It is implied that these directories have separate file permissions.

5.2 Linux Namespace Isolation

Problem

You want to use Linux namespaces so that processes are fully isolated.

Solution

Configure the application to use Linux namespace isolation:

```
{
    "applications": {
        "auth-service": {
            "type": "php",
            ...
            "isolation": {
                "namespaces": {
                    "cgroup": true,
                    "credential": true,
                    "mount": true,
                    "network": true,
                    "pid": true,
                    "uname": true
                },
                "uidmap": [
                    {
                        "host": 1000,
                        "container": 0,
                        "size": 1000
                    }
                ],
```

```
                "gidmap": [
                    {
                        "host": 1000,
                        "container": 0,
                        "size": 1000
                    }
                ],
                "rootfs": "/var/app/sandbox/"
            }
        }
    }
}
```

This example exercises all of the available Linux namespace configurations for an NGINX Unit application.

Discussion

A Linux namespace wraps a global system resource in an abstraction that makes it appear to the processes within the namespace that they have their own isolated instance of the global resource. Changes to the global resource are visible to other processes that are members of the namespace but are invisible to other processes.

This NGINX Unit feature provides your application with an isolated runtime environment native to the underlying operating system. This type of isolation is akin to Docker and LXC, as they use Linux namespaces and cgroups to separate containers. This isolation is available on Linux systems and may not be fully supported by every OS that NGINX Unit is capable of running on, such as FreeBSD, MacOS, and Solaris. The uidmap and gidmap options are available only if the operating system supports Linux user namespaces.

The rootfs option provides the ability to confine the application in a directory. This feature enables Linux chroot abilities of NGINX Unit.

Additional Resources

Linux Namespaces (*https://oreil.ly/DLxvR*)
Cgroup Namespaces (*https://oreil.ly/lhqYN*)
User Namespaces (*https://oreil.ly/5sSl4*)
Mount Namespaces (*https://oreil.ly/U5g9A*)
Network Namespaces (*https://oreil.ly/lMvDY*)
PID Namespaces (*https://oreil.ly/O1zjk*)
Uname Namespaces (*https://oreil.ly/4m15j*)
chroot Man Page (*https://oreil.ly/YA4ab*)

5.3 API Security Through Encryption

Problem

You need to secure your application's communication with SSL/TLS certificates.

Solution

Create a `.pem` file that includes your certificate chain and private key:

```
cat cert.pem ca.pem key.pem | sudo tee bundle.pem > /dev/null
```

Upload the *bundle.pem* file to Unit's certificate storage under a suitable name:

```
sudo curl -X PUT --data-binary @bundle.pem \
        --unix-socket /var/run/control.unit.socket \
        http://localhost/certificates/certificate-name
```

Configure a listener object to use the certificate. In this example, a file with the object will be written to a file named *tls-listener.json* for clarity:

```
{
    "*:8443": {
        "pass": "applications/app-name",
        "tls": {
            "certificate": "certificate-name"
        }
    }
}
```

Submit the *tls-listener.json* configuration to the Unit API:

```
sudo curl -X PUT -d @tls-listener.json \
        --unix-socket /var/run/control.unit.socket \
        http://localhost/config/listeners
```

This command removes all other listeners that might have been defined previously.

Validate that your application is communicating over TLS:

```
curl -v https://localhost:8443
```

Discussion

This recipe concatenates the certificate, certificate authority chain, and key into a bundle that can be used by NGINX Unit. After the certificate is uploaded to Unit's certificate store, it can be referenced by listeners. A listener object is constructed using the IP and port on which to accept requests. It references the application via the pass attribute, as well as the certificate bundle object. The listener object is then submitted to the Unit control interface.

Validating that the TLS certificate is configured properly can be done by making a request to the listener. Using the verbose flag, -v, when issuing the curl command will print the TLS handshake operations if the certificate is configured properly.

Additional Resources

TLS Object (*http://bit.ly/2UBy1an*)

CHAPTER 6

Application Integration

To provide examples of serving real-world applications with NGINX Unit, this chapter will demonstrate step-by-step setups of some common application frameworks. In this chapter, you will learn how to serve WordPress, a common PHP content management system. You will also learn how to serve applications based in common frameworks such as Django, Flask (Python frameworks), and Express (a Node.js framework). A Ruby example is also provided, making use of the common framework Ruby on Rails. This chapter will demonstrate how to install applications onto a system and ensure that they have the correct file permissions and the configuration of NGINX Unit needed to serve them.

6.1 WordPress

Problem

You need to run WordPress with NGINX Unit.

Solution

To install WordPress (*http://bit.ly/2IGsBt4*), if you haven't already done so, check the prerequisites (*https://oreil.ly/eAACv*) to ensure that you have the necessary requirements. Next, configure the WordPress database (*https://oreil.ly/W5Vew*). Then download and extract the WordPress files:

```
sudo mkdir /var/app/
sudo cd /var/app/
sudo wget https://wordpress.org/latest.tar.gz
sudo tar xzvf latest.tar.gz
```

In this example, the WordPress files will be stored in */var/app/wordpress/*.

Update (*https://oreil.ly/l7Lzn*) the *wp-config.php* file with your database settings and other customizations.

Set the user file permissions (*http://bit.ly/2GFqzFY*) for WordPress to ensure that the user that owns the PHP processes and the user running the Unit server are able to access the files:

```
sudo chown -R wpuser:www-data /var/app/wordpress/
sudo find /var/app/wordpress/ -type d -exec chmod g+s {} \;
sudo chmod g+w /var/app/wordpress/wp-content
sudo chmod -R g+w /var/app/wordpress/wp-content/themes
sudo chmod -R g+w /var/app/wordpress/wp-content/plugins
```

Configure a PHP application object, as well as a listener object, and submit both objects to the NGINX Unit control interface. This example will configure two applications and listeners in order to isolate the main WordPress entry point, *index.php*, from the rest of the PHP files that can be run, such as *wp-admin.php*. Name the following JSON file *wordpress-unit.json*:

```
{
    "listeners": {
        "*:8080": {
            "pass": "routes/wordpress"
        }
    },
    "routes": {
        "wordpress": [
            {
                "match": {
                    "uri": [
                        "*.php",
                        "*.php/*",
                        "/wp-admin/"
                    ]
                },
                "action": {
                    "pass": "applications/wordpress/direct"
                }
            },
            {
                "action": {
                    "share": "/var/app/wordpress/",
                    "fallback": {
                        "pass": "applications/wordpress/index"
                    }
                }
            }
        ]
    },
    "applications": {
        "wordpress": {
            "type": "php",
```

```
        "user": "wpuser",
        "group": "www-data",
        "targets": {
            "direct": {
                "root": "/path/to/wordpress/"
            },
            "index": {
                "root": "/path/to/wordpress/",
                "script": "index.php"
            }
        }
    }
}
}
```

Submit the *wordpress-unit.json* file to the Unit control interface:

```
sudo curl -X PUT -d @wordpress-unit.json \
    --unix-socket /var/run/control.unit.socket \
    http://localhost/config
```

Use a browser to make a request to Unit on port 8080, and finish the installation (*https://oreil.ly/UR3qZ*) process.

Discussion

In this recipe, WordPress is installed from scratch. The system and database first need to be prepared to WordPress specifications. After the system is prepared, the code base is downloaded and unpacked to a location on the filesystem.

Once the application code is on the filesystem, WordPress needs to be informed how to connect to the database. This is done by altering a configuration file that is included in the code base. For the sake of brevity, this is statically configured. In a production system, environment variables would be used and set when configuring the Unit application.

After the database connection has been configured, the file permissions are changed so that the system user that will own the Unit processes will be able to read the files. Permissions are also set for the system group.

When configuring Unit to serve the application, a route is used to send any requests that specify a filename ending with .php or a file path that starts with /wp-admin/, directly to the application script. All other requests are attempted to be served statically. If a static file is not found, the request is directed to the main index.php script.

Additional Resources

WordPress How-To (*http://bit.ly/2IICgz7*)

6.2 Django

Problem

You have a Python Django application you want to serve with NGINX Unit.

Solution

Prepare your existing project or create a new one (*http://bit.ly/2Dxresg*). NGINX Unit looks for a callable entity within the WSGI module provided, named `application`. In this example, the source code will be placed in */var/project/*. Start by ensuring that the correct file permissions are set:

```
sudo chown -R app-user /var/project/
```

Detailing the directory structure of the example is important because Unit needs to know how to import the WSGI module in order to run the application. Thus the Unit application object values depend on the directory structure:

```
/var/project/
├── manage.py
├── app1/
│   └── ...
├── app2/
│   └── ...
├── static/
│   └── ...
└── project/
    ├── ...
    └── wsgi.py
```

Construct an NGINX Unit Python application object and associated listener. Name this file *django-unit.json*:

```
{
    "listeners": {
        "127.0.0.1:8080": {
            "pass": "routes"
        }
    },

    "routes": [
        {
            "match": {
                "uri": "/static/*"
            },
            "action": {
                "share": "/var/project/"
            }
        },
        {
```

```
            "action": {
                "pass": "applications/django_project"
            }
        }
    ],

    "applications": {
        "django_project": {
            "type": "python",
            "path": "/var/project/",
            "home": "/path/to/virtual-env/if/used/",
            "module": "project.wsgi",
            "user": "app-user"
        }
    }
}
```

Submit the *django-unit.json* file to the Unit control interface:

```
sudo curl -X PUT -d @django-unit.json \
    --unix-socket /var/run/control.unit.socket \
    http://localhost/config
```

Validate that the application is running by making a request to the server on port 8080:

```
curl http://localhost:8080
```

Discussion

In this recipe, a Django project is served with NGINX Unit. In order for Unit application processes to read the files, appropriate file permissions must be set. In the example, the files are owned by the system user that will be running the application.

This recipe shows the directory structure, not because it needs to be followed but because it shows how the module attribute of the Unit application object for Python applications is configured. The value of the module attribute is used to import the WSGI module, with standard Python import syntax, from the directory specified by the path attribute.

The Unit configuration specifies that this application is of type python. As the version of Python is not specified, the latest version is used. The path attribute specifies the path to the base directory of the application. If a virtual environment is being used, the optional home attribute can be set to the base directory of the virtual environment. Unit imports the WSGI object by use of the module attribute and runs the application as specified by the system user.

The configuration also defines a listener object that instructs Unit to send incoming requests on the 127.0.0.1:8080 interface, to be processed by the routes configuration. A route is defined to match the URI, /static/*, and serve static files from the root directory of the project. As the URI path must be prefixed with `/static/`, only files in the *static* directory will be matched. All other requests will be directed to the `django_project` application.

Additional Resources

Django How-To (*http://bit.ly/2UHg8Xq*)

6.3 Flask

Problem

You have a Python Flask application you want to serve with NGINX Unit.

Solution

Prepare your existing project. NGINX Unit looks for a callable entity within the WSGI module provided, named `application`. In many Flask examples, the Flask application is initiated and simply called `app`. If this is the case with your project, you'll have to make alterations. The following is the most minimal amount of code we can provide to run a Flask application and have it ready to be served by NGINX Unit. For this example, the name of the file will be simply called *app.py*:

```
from flask import Flask
application = Flask(__name__)

@application.route('/')
def hello_world():
    return 'Hello, Unit!'
```

In this example, the source code will be placed in */var/project/*. Start by ensuring that the correct file permissions are set:

```
sudo chown -R app-user /var/project/
```

Construct an NGINX Unit Python application object and associated listener. Name this file *flask-unit.json*:

```
{
    "listeners": {
        "127.0.0.1:8080": {
            "pass": "applications/flask_project"
        }
    },

    "applications": {
        "flask_project": {
            "type": "python",
            "path": "/var/project/",
```

```
            "home": "/path/to/virtual-env/if/used/",
            "module": "app",
            "user": "app-user"
        }
    }
}
```

Submit the *flask-unit.json* file to the Unit control interface:

```
sudo curl -X PUT -d @flask-unit.json \
        --unix-socket /var/run/control.unit.socket \
        http://localhost/config
```

Validate that the application is running by making a request to the server on port 8080:

```
curl http://localhost:8080
```

Discussion

In this recipe, a Flask project is served with NGINX Unit. For Unit to be permitted to read the files, the correct file permissions need to be set. In the example, the files are owned by the system user that will be running the application.

The Unit configuration specifies that this application is of type python. As the version of Python is not specified, the latest version is used. The path attribute specifies the path to the base directory of the application. If a virtual environment is being used, the optional home attribute can be set to the base directory of the virtual environment. Unit imports the file that contains the Flask application object by use of the module attribute and runs the application as specified by the system user. As noted previously, it's important that this object be explicitly named application. The configuration then defines a listener object that instructs Unit to send incoming requests on the 127.0.0.1:8080 interface, to be directed to the flask_project application.

Additional Resources

Flask How-To (*https://unit.nginx.org/howto/flask*)
Flask Quickstart (*https://flask.palletsprojects.com/en/1.1.x/quickstart*)

6.4 Express

Problem

You have a Node.js application that utilizes the Express framework.

Solution

Set up your project and ensure that Node is installed (*http://bit.ly/2vnJa4i*).

To run Node applications in NGINX Unit, an NPM package is required. The version of the NPM package unit-http must match the version of NGINX Unit being used. It's wise to version-lock the Unit server and the NPM package to avoid version conflicts. To build and install the NPM package, you will first need the Unit development package, which includes necessary header files. The Unit development package is installed via the system package manager and was shown in the installation process in Chapter 2:

```
npm install unit-http
```

Unit will call the Node application's entry point as an executable. Add the following line to the beginning of the entry point file:

```
#!/usr/bin/env node
```

Make the entry point executable, and ensure that it can be executed by the system user that will run the application. In the example, the entry point file is *index.js*, and the project directory is */var/app/*:

```
chown -R app-user /var/app/
chmod u+x index.js
```

To serve an Express application with Unit, the code needs to be modified slightly. The default Express HTTP server, ServerResponse, and IncomingMessage objects need to be replaced with objects from the default http package to the unit-http package. The following "Hello World!" example shows how to rewire the application:

```
#!/usr/bin/env node

const {
  createServer,
  IncomingMessage,
  ServerResponse,
} = require('unit-http')

require('http').ServerResponse = ServerResponse
require('http').IncomingMessage = IncomingMessage

const express = require('express')

const app = express()

app.get('/', (req, res) => {
  res.set('X-Header-Example', 'Value')
  res.send('Hello, Unit!')
})

createServer(app).listen()
```

NGINX Unit also supports the WebSocket protocol; your Node.js app only needs to replace the default websocket with:

```
var webSocketServer = require('unit-http/websocket').server;
```

Construct the NGINX Unit application and listener objects for this project and name the file *express-unit.json*:

```
{
    "listeners": {
        "127.0.0.1:8080": {
            "pass": "applications/express_project"
        }
    },

    "applications": {
        "express_project": {
            "type": "external",
            "executable": "/var/app/index.js",
            "user": "app-user"
        }
    }
}
```

Submit the *express-unit.json* file to the Unit control interface:

```
sudo curl -X PUT -d @express-unit.json \
        --unix-socket /var/run/control.unit.socket \
        http://localhost/config
```

Validate that the application is running by making a request to the server on port 8080.

Discussion

In this recipe, the unit-http package is installed to the project, and its objects are used rather than the default http server objects. The entry point file is made executable and the correct file permissions are set on the project so that Unit is able to read the modules and run the entry point. Lastly, the Unit application and listener objects are constructed and submitted to the Unit control API. The executable attribute specifies the location of the entry point file. An optional application object attribute for external application types, named arguments, can be used if there are arguments that need to be passed to the executable.

Additional Resources

Express How-To (*http://bit.ly/2VriBd9*)

6.5 Ruby

Problem

You have a Ruby application you want to serve with NGINX Unit.

Solution

Install the `rack` Ruby gem:

```
$ gem install rack
```

Construct an NGINX Unit Ruby application object and associated listener. Name this
file *ruby-unit.json*:

```
{
    "listeners": {
        "127.0.0.1:8080": {
            "pass": "applications/ruby_app"
        }
    },

    "applications": {
        "ruby_app": {
            "type": "ruby",
            "processes": 5,
            "script": "/www/app/config.ru",
            "working_directory": "/var/app/"
        }
    }
}
```

Submit the *ruby-unit.json* file to the Unit control interface:

```
sudo curl -X PUT -d @ruby-unit.json \
     --unix-socket /var/run/control.unit.socket \
     http://localhost/config
```

Validate that the application is running by making a request to the server on port
8080:

```
curl http://localhost:8080
```

Discussion

In this recipe, a Ruby application is served with NGINX Unit. To run Ruby scripts,
Unit uses the `rack` interface to run Ruby scripts, which is why its installation was
called out. The only required attribute of a Unit Ruby application object is `script`.
The `script` attribute specifies the path to the application entry point. In Ruby on

---

Rails projects, this script is at the base of the project initiated by the `rails new app-name` command and is called *config.ru*.

The Unit configuration specifies that this application is of type `ruby`. The `script` attribute specifies the full path to the applications entry point, sets the number of `pro cesses` to 5, and sets the `working_directory` to `/var/app/`. The configuration then defines a listener object that instructs Unit to send incoming requests on the `127.0.0.1:8080` interface, to be directed to the `ruby_app` application.

Additional Resources

Ruby on Rails Getting Started (*https://guides.rubyonrails.org/getting_started.html*)
NGINX Unit Redmine Example (*https://unit.nginx.org/howto/redmine*)

CHAPTER 7

Ecosystem Integration

Throughout this chapter, you will learn about operational integration as it pertains to NGINX Unit. Unit applications may need to be served via an NGINX proxy or load balancer, to which the configuration will be detailed. Also included are recipes that enable you to securely expose the Unit control interface through NGINX. Other topics include running Unit within a container and deploying application version upgrades through the control API.

7.1 Reverse Proxying to Unit Applications Through NGINX

Problem

You need to serve an application running in NGINX Unit through an NGINX server acting as a reverse proxy or load balancer.

Solution

Configure an `upstream` block in the NGINX configuration made up of Unit servers:

```
upstream unit_backend {
    server 127.0.0.1:8080; # Local Reverse Proxy
    server 10.0.0.12:8080; # Remote Server Load Balance
    server 10.0.1.12:8080; # Remote Server Load Balance
}
```

Configure a `server` block within the NGINX configuration to proxy requests to the `upstream` server set:

```
server {
    # Typical NGINX server setup and security directives

    location / {
```

```
    # NGINX Proxy Settings
    proxy_pass http://unit_backend;
  }
}
```

Discussion

The NGINX web server and reverse proxy load balancer is a fully dynamic application gateway. It can be used as a web server, reverse proxy, load balancer, and more. For brevity, this recipe assumes that the NGINX server block has been configured with the necessary required and security-concerned directives.

In a reverse proxy situation, the NGINX server would be configured on the same physical or virtual machine as NGINX Unit. The upstream block would be configured with a server directive with a parameter specifying the same interface configured for the Unit listener object. In this example, the localhost 127.0.0.1 is used in conjunction with the port 8080.

In a load balancing situation, the NGINX server would be configured with an upstream block that contains multiple remote server directives. The example provides two server directives specifying different remote NGINX Unit servers at IP addresses 10.0.0.12 and 10.0.1.12. Both of these Unit servers would be configured with listener objects on port 8080 for the same application.

This example further demonstrates how a properly configured server block can receive connections and direct the request to the upstream block. This is done by defining a location block and using the proxy_pass directive with a parameter that specifies the protocol and destination. In this example, the destination is the upstream server block, named unit_backend.

Incoming connections to the NGINX server will be processed, and requests matching the configured server definition will be directed to the configuration within this server block. In this example, all configuration requests will be sent to the NGINX Unit server for processing. The NGINX Unit server will return the request to the NGINX server, which will return the request to the client.

Additional Resources

NGINX Integration (*http://bit.ly/2XDCYkA*)

7.2 Securely Serving the NGINX Unit Control API

Problem

You would like to remotely and securely configure the Unit application server.

Solution

Configure an NGINX reverse proxy to the control interface Unix socket. Ensure that it is available only internally and that client-server encryption is enforced:

```
server {

    # Configure SSL encryption
    server 443 ssl;
    ssl_certificate /path/to/ssl/cert.pem;
    ssl_certificate_key /path/to/ssl/cert.key;

    # Configure SSL client certificate validation
    ssl_client_certificate /path/to/ca.pem;
    ssl_verify_client on;

    # Configure network ACLs
    #allow 1.2.3.4; # Uncomment and update with the IP addresses
                    # and networks of your administrative systems.
    deny all;

    # Configure HTTP Basic authentication
    auth_basic on;
    auth_basic_user_file /path/to/htpasswd;

    location / {
        proxy_pass http://unix:/var/run/control.unit.sock;
    }
}
```

Discussion

This recipe configures the NGINX reverse proxy server to serve the NGINX Unit control interface through an HTTPS connection. The NGINX server is configured to serve only on port 443 and to accept only encrypted connections. The SSL/TLS directives of the NGINX server must be configured to specify a given certificate and key for encryption. This configuration also requires the client to provide a certificate signed by the specified certificate authority as a means of authentication. For further security, the configuration denies all requests from any client IP that is not specified by the allow directive. The allow directive must be uncommented and configured to your internal IP or CIDR. Finally, a username and password must be specified via HTTP basic auth. The auth_basic_user_file directive defines a file that contains usernames and hashed passwords of authorized users.

Once all security measures are met, NGINX will proxy the request to the NGINX Unit control interface. By default, the Unit control interface listens on a Unix socket. The system user running NGINX must have permission to read and write to this Unix socket file.

Additional Resources

NGINX Integration (*http://bit.ly/2XDCYkA*)

7.3 Containerized Environment

Problem

You would like to use NGINX Unit as a middleware server in a containerized environment.

Solution

Build a unit configuration file at the base of the project. Name the file *unit-conf.json*:

```
{
    "listeners": {
        "*:8080": {
            "pass": "applications/php_project"
        }
    },
    "applications": {
        "php_project": {
            "type": "php",
            "processes": 1,
            "root": "/var/app",
            "index": "index.php"
        }
    }
}
```

Use the Official NGINX Unit Docker Image as the base. Create a Dockerfile with the following:

```
FROM nginx/unit

ADD / /var/app/

ADD /unit-conf.json /docker-entrypoint.d/
```

Build the Dockerfile into an image:

```
docker build -t unit-example
```

Run the Docker image and expose the listener through the Docker proxy for testing. The following example uses the Docker -p flag to configure a proxy, exposing port 8080 proxied to port 8080. As a reminder, the port number before the : is the port exposed on the local machine:

```
docker run -p 8080:8080 unit-example
```

Make a request to the exposed Docker proxy to validate:

```
curl localhost:8080
```

Discussion

This recipe demonstrates the basics of using NGINX Unit as a middleware server for dockerized applications. A Unit configuration file is created for the application. A Dockerfile is then crafted, based on the Official NGINX Unit Docker Image. Within the Dockerfile, the application code is added to the image. The configuration file is then added to the image at the location /docker-entrypoint.d/.

The /docker-entrypoint.d/ location enables Unit to bootstrap the container with SSL/TLS certificates or Unit configuration snippets and allows for arbitrary code execution. Files with the extension .pem will be uploaded as certificates, .json as Unit configuration. Arbitrary scripts with the .sh extension will run after certificates and configurations are uploaded to Unit.

The Dockerfile is then built, rendering an image tagged unit-example. The Docker image is then run with the proxy flag to expose the listener to the host. Once running, the Docker container is validated.

Furthermore, with Docker you can mount volumes with the -v flag. Doing so enables you to expose the host's filesystem. If the control interface is overridden via the CMD directive in the Dockerfile, and exposed by the Docker proxy, remote reconfiguration of the Unit container is enabled. In this configuration it is possible to add applications that exist on the host's filesystem and to reconfigure Unit listeners to serve these applications remotely through the control API. This technique may be helpful for local development environments.

Additional Resources

Unit in Docker (*http://bit.ly/2UGUrXw*)

7.4 Deployments

Problem

You need to deploy a new version of an application without downtime.

Solution

Utilize NGINX Unit's API to switch between application versions through an API call. This recipe will use a directory structure laid out in the following way:

```
/var/app/
├── version-1
│   ├── index.php
│   └── ...
└── version-2
    ├── index.php
    └── ...
```

The current state of the Unit configuration is as follows:

```
{
    "listeners": {
        "*:8080": {
            "pass": "applications/php_project_version_1"
        }
    },
    "applications": {
        "php_project_version_1": {
            "type": "php",
            "processes": 2,
            "root": "/var/app/version-1",
            "index": "index.php"
        }
    }
}
```

Create another file named *php-v2.json* file with the following JSON:

```
{
    "type": "php",
    "processes": 2,
    "root": "/var/app/version-2",
    "index": "index.php"
}
```

Make an API call to the control interface. Provide the *php-v2.json* as the JSON body. Use the RESTful syntax to name the Unit application php_project_version_2:

```
sudo curl -X PUT -d @php-v2.json \
    --unix-socket /var/run/control.unit.sock \
    http://localhost/config/applications/php_project_version_2
```

Make the following request to the Unit control interface to validate that both applications are configured:

```
sudo curl --unix-socket /var/run/control.unit.sock \
    http://localhost/config
{
    "listeners": {
        "*:8080": {
            "pass": "applications/php_project_version_1"
        }
    },
```

```
            "applications": {
                    "php_project_version_1": {
                            "type": "php",
                            "processes": 2,
                            "root": "/var/app/version-1",
                            "index": "index.php"
                    },

                    "php_project_version_2": {
                            "type": "php",
                            "processes": 2,
                            "root": "/var/app/version-2",
                            "index": "index.php"
                    }
            }
    }
```

Make a request to the control interface with the following command, instructing Unit to switch the listener *:8080 to point to the php_project_version_2 application:

```
sudo curl -X PUT -d '"php_project_version_2"' \
    --unix-socket /var/run/control.unit.sock \
    'http://localhost/config/listeners/*:8080/application'
```

Make the following request to the Unit control interface to validate that the listener has been reconfigured to direct requests to the php_project_version_2 application:

```
sudo curl --unix-socket /var/run/control.unit.sock \
    http://localhost/config
{
    "listeners": {
        "*:8080": {
            "pass": "applications/php_project_version_2"
        }
    },

    "applications": {
        "php_project_version_1": {
            "type": "php",
            "processes": 2,
            "root": "/var/app/version-1",
            "index": "index.php"
        },

        "php_project_version_2": {
            "type": "php",
            "processes": 2,
            "root": "/var/app/version-2",
            "index": "index.php"
        }
    }
}
```

Make a request to the control interface to remove the `php_project_version_1` application:

```
sudo curl -X DELETE \
     --unix-socket /var/run/control.unit.sock \
     http://localhost/config/applications/php_project_version_1
```

Discussion

This recipe demonstrates the deployment of a new version of an application. The example starts from a preconfigured state, with a single application version being served on port 8080. NGINX Unit is then configured to start another application of a new version. Both versions run in parallel as separate process sets. Unit is then instructed to route incoming requests to the new application version. Finally, the older application version is removed, and the processes that served that application are removed.

Conclusion

This book focused on the NGINX Unit server, its capabilities, its configuration, and where it fits in your system architecture. By working through these recipes, you've gained a working knowledge of installing NGINX Unit and Unit's configuration elements, and you've tackled real-world examples of serving different applications.

I personally find Unit useful because of its simplistic configuration and powerful versatility. Using a single middleware server to run multiple applications that are written in different languages and configured dynamically via an API enables me to move quickly and rely on common methodologies for all web applications. It is my hope that this book has provided you with the ability to effectively manage NGINX Unit in your web application landscape.

Index

About the Author

Derek DeJonghe has had a lifelong passion for technology. His background and experience in web development, system administration, and networking give him a well-rounded understanding of modern web architecture. Derek leads a team of site reliability and cloud solution engineers and produces self-healing, auto-scaling infrastructure for numerous applications. While designing, building, and maintaining highly available applications for clients, he consults for larger organizations as they embark on their journey to the cloud. Derek and his team are on the forefront of a technology tidal wave and are engineering cloud best practices every day. With a proven track record for resilient cloud architecture, Derek pioneers cloud deployments for security and maintainability that are in the best interest of his clients.

Colophon

The animal on the cover of *NGINX Unit Cookbook* is an African wildcat (*Felis lybica*), a species of wildcat native to Africa, west and southern Asia, and parts of Europe.

While similar in size and appearance to its house cat relative, the African wildcat has red-orange ears and long hind legs that give the cat a distinctive upright posture when seated. It is estimated that the wildcat was first domesticated about ten thousand years ago, based on the discovery of wildcat remains buried with Neolithic farmers.

This cat has a sandy brown or gray, short coat with faint tabby stripes and black rings on its tapered tail. Other identifying markings typically include an orange spot around the nose and white patches below the eyes.

The African wildcat is mainly active at night, hunting insects, rodents, birds, and reptiles. Although mostly a solitary species, temporary packs comprised of a female with her offspring from several litters can form, depending on prey availability in the surrounding territory.

While the African wildcat's conservation status is currently listed as of Least Concern, cross-breeding with domestic cats has a significant impact on this species' wild population. Many of the animals on O'Reilly covers are endangered; all of them are important to the world.

The cover illustration is by Karen Montgomery, based on a black and white engraving from *Dover*. The cover fonts are Gilroy Semibold and Guardian Sans. The text font is Adobe Minion Pro; the heading font is Adobe Myriad Condensed; and the code font is Dalton Maag's Ubuntu Mono.

O'REILLY®

There's much more
where this came from.

Experience books, videos, live online
training courses, and more from O'Reilly
and our 200+ partners—all in one place.

Learn more at oreilly.com/online-learning